I Can Read About
FOSSILS

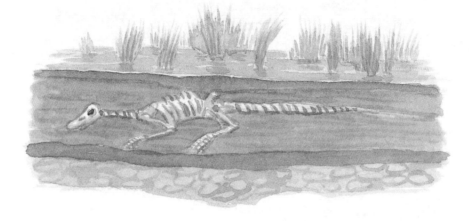

Written by John Howard • Illustrated by Lisa Bonforte

Consultant: Dr. Niles Eldredge, Curator
Department of Invertebrates, American Museum of Natural History

Troll

Millions of years ago, giant creatures called dinosaurs and other prehistoric animals ruled the earth. Our planet was a very different place then. For many years the air was warmer, and much of the land was low and swampy.

Trachodon

During that time, the swamps were filled with plant-eating dinosaurs, such as Brachiosaurus (BRAK-ee-uh-sawr-us) and Trachodon (TRAK-uh-don).

Brachiosaurus

Fierce meat-eating dinosaurs,
like Allosaurus (AL-uh-sawr-us)
and Tyrannosaurus (tie-RAN-
uh-sawr-us), chased after the
smaller dinosaurs. Large
plant-eaters like Diplodocus
(dih-PLOD-uh-kus) were
also the prey of the
meat-eaters.

Diplodocus

Imagine how the ground shook when Tyrannosaurus fought the three-horned plant-eater Triceratops (tri-SER-uh-tops).

Tyrannosaurus

Triceratops

Long ago, even the air was filled with strange creatures, such as the flying pterodactyl (ter-uh-DAK-til).

In the sea swam strange-looking fish and sea serpents with razor-sharp teeth.

For more than 100 million years, the dinosaurs and other prehistoric creatures ruled the earth. Then they mysteriously died out and became extinct.

Why did they vanish from the earth? No one is sure.

Some scientists think that a giant meteorite crashed into the earth, raising huge clouds of dust that blocked out the sun. Without any sun, the earth may have become too cold for the dinosaurs. Perhaps they could not adapt, or change, to the cooler climate. Without sunlight, plants would not have been able to grow. Then there would not be any food for the plant-eating dinosaurs to eat. And if the plant-eaters died out, the meat-eaters would not have food either.

Other scientists think volcanoes may have erupted throughout the world, sending clouds of ash into the air. Again, without sunlight, plants would die out. Without enough to eat, the dinosaurs would also have died out.

Although many scientists believe birds are related to dinosaurs, none of the ancient dinosaurs are alive today. Yet we know a lot about these creatures. We know what many of them looked like, what they ate, and where some of them lived. How do we know these things?

The dinosaurs left clues that tell us a great deal. These clues
are called *fossils*. Fossils are bones, teeth, footprints, and impressions
of animals and plants that lived long ago.

Fossils are usually found in sedimentary (sed-uh-MEN-tuh-ree) rocks. Sedimentary rocks are rocks such as sandstone, shale, and limestone. They are formed when mud, sand, clay, and minerals pile up in layers. These layers are pressed together for millions of years, and they eventually turn to rock.

Sandstone

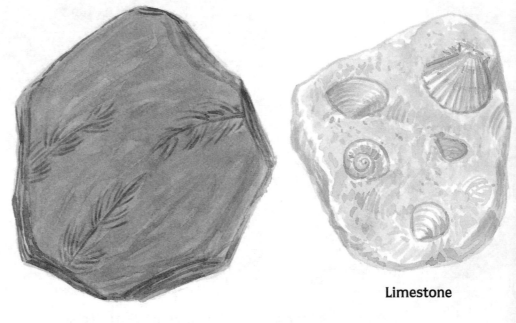

Shale

Limestone

When the dinosaurs died, many of them sank to the bottom of swamps or rivers that existed long ago. In time, all that was left of these dinosaurs were their bones. The bones were covered with layers of mud and sand that later turned to rock.

A paleontologist (pale-ee-on-TOL-uh-just) is a scientist who studies fossils. Paleontologists are like detectives. They follow the clues that solve the mystery of the dinosaurs. Fossils are the keys to unlocking these secrets of the past.

Knowing where to look for fossils is important. But even when scientists know *where* to look, fossils are not always easy to find. It can take days, months, and years of searching to find even the smallest fossils.

A fossil hunter must carefully remove layers of rock with a strong steel hammer and a chisel. Or, if the stone around the fossil is crumbly, a brush may be used. A small bone might be found right away. That bone is carefully wrapped in tissue paper or newspaper to protect it. Then the search continues—one bone means that others might be hidden nearby.

Sometimes, if fossil hunters are lucky, they find entire skeletons. But most of the time, they find only small pieces, which must be put together like the pieces of a giant jigsaw puzzle.

Scientists are not the only people who find fossils. Almost 200 years ago in England, a 12-year-old girl found something very strange. It was a complete skeleton of a 7-foot-long (2-meter-long) creature trapped in rock. It looked as if it were part fish and part lizard. Scientists decided to call it Ichthyosaurus (ik-thee-uh-SAWR-us), which means "fish lizard."

Thanks to that young girl's discovery, today we have a good idea of how Ichthyosaurus looked.

The same girl later discovered two other fossil skeletons. One was a sea serpent called Plesiosaurus (PLEE-see-uh-SAWR-us).

Plesiosaurus

The other was a flying reptile
called a pterosaur (TER-uh-sawr).

Pterosaur

Fossils of other flying reptiles have been found in Texas and Kansas. Buried in rock were several skeletons of prehistoric, birdlike creatures. The wings of these animals were nearly 30 feet (9 meters) wide.

In Montana and Wyoming, scientists found enough bones to put together two full Tyrannosaurus skeletons. Tyrannosaurus was 20 feet (6 meters) tall and 49 feet (15 meters) long.

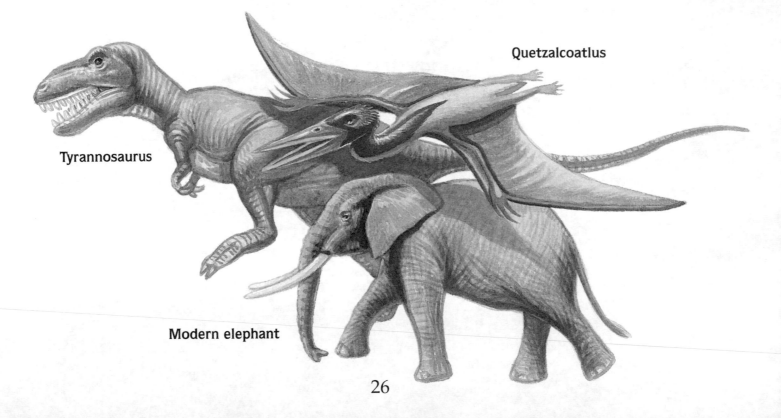

Quetzalcoatlus

Tyrannosaurus

Modern elephant

Most of the time, though, fossilized animals are not found as complete skeletons. But if enough bones are found, scientists can fill in the missing parts with plaster bones. Then, they can put the skeleton back together again.

One of the most exciting fossil treasures was found in the Gobi Desert in Mongolia. Nestled among sandstone rocks was an entire nest of dinosaur eggs.

Flaming Cliffs, Gobi Desert

The eggs belonged to the Oviraptor (oh-vee-RAP-tur) dinosaur. Skeletons of this ostrich-sized creature are often found in the Flaming Cliffs.

Oviraptor's eggs were shaped like potatoes, and each was about 8 inches (20 centimeters) long. Inside were the fossilized remains of baby dinosaurs.

Besides dinosaur fossils, scientists also look for the fossils of other kinds of animals. Prehistoric mammals that lived thousands of years ago, such as the mammoth, saber-toothed tiger, giant sloth, and giant bison, were huge and ferocious. The fossils of many of these mammals have been found in the La Brea Tar Pits of California.

Scientists think that shallow water covered the tops of the tar pits in prehistoric times. When the animals came to drink, they stepped into the water and were trapped by the sticky tar. Unable to escape, they died there, and the tar fossilized their skeletons.

Over 1,000 saber-toothed tigers' skulls, as well as many bones, tusks, and teeth, have been pulled out of the tar pits.

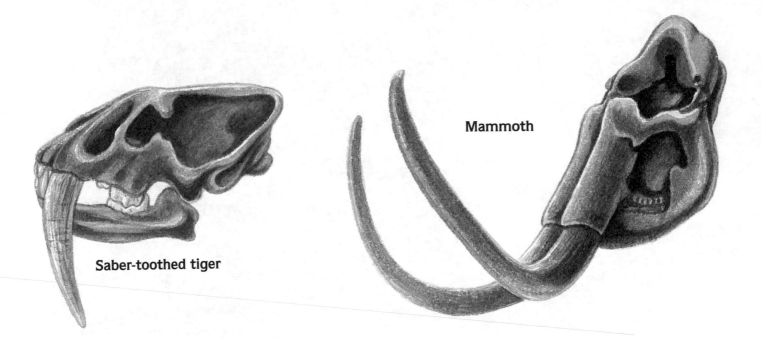

Saber-toothed tiger

Mammoth

Another startling discovery was made in 1901 by a hunter who was walking across the frozen wilderness of Siberia. Suddenly, he saw something very strange! A huge, hairy elephant over 13 feet (4 meters) tall, with long curved tusks, was standing in a snow drift. The hunter was looking at a giant mammoth that had died thousands of years ago. It was perfectly preserved— frozen solid in ice and snow.

Other types of fossils are impressions of plants and small animals found in rocks or coal. Sometimes, scientists find insects or plants in amber. Amber is fossilized tree sap. Long ago, insects or bits of plants were trapped in the sticky tree sap. When the sap hardened and turned to amber, the insects and plants were perfectly preserved.

Insects and plants in amber

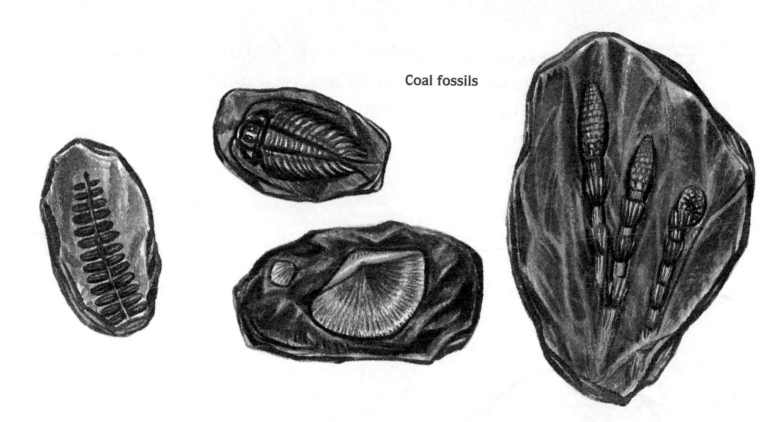

Coal fossils

Coal is called a fossil fuel. As ancient plants and prehistoric forests sank into the earth, they hardened into layers and fossilized. The heat and pressure of the earth changed these plants and trees into coal. Fossil imprints of small animals are often found in coal formed hundreds of millions of years ago.

Fossil impressions can tell us what life was like on earth. Such impressions show the shapes of plants that lived millions of years ago. By studying past plant life, scientists can also tell what the climate was like then.

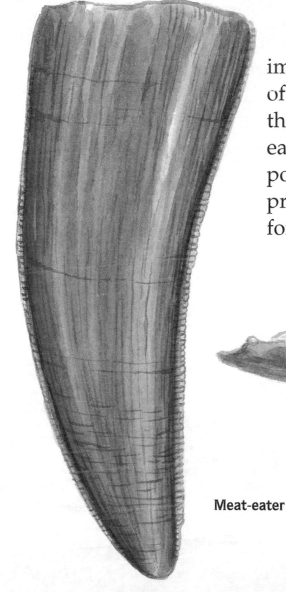

Every fossil, no matter how small, is important. By studying the size and shape of fossil teeth, for example, we can tell if the animal was a meat-eater or a plant-eater. Many meat-eaters had sharp, pointed teeth for tearing the flesh of their prey. The plant-eaters often had flat teeth for grinding their food.

Plant-eater

Meat-eater

37

When fossils of sea creatures or fossil shells are found on dry land, scientists know that the dry land was probably covered with water in prehistoric times. Fossil shells often give us other clues to the past. For example, if the fossil shell of a creature that lives in warm water is found in a cold climate, we know the climate has changed from warm to cold.

How can scientists tell how old a fossil is? One way is by measuring the amount of radioactive elements in the ancient lava found above and below a fossil. Knowing this, scientists are able to calculate how old the fossil is. Scientists also study the layers of rock where fossils are found. This is because different layers of rock were formed at different times in the earth's past, with the lower layers being older than the layers above them. This means fossils found in the higher layers are younger than those in the lower levels.

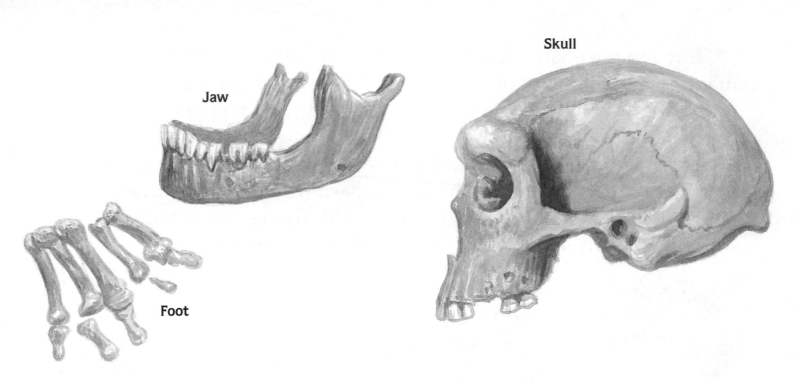

Jaw

Skull

Foot

The search for information about the past goes on. Perhaps the most interesting fossils are human fossils. They help tell us the story of early humans.

Long after the dinosaurs died out, early humans developed. What did early people look like? Did they use tools? Did they know how to use fire? Fossils help tell the story and give us clues to the past.

An important discovery was made in the Italian Alps in 1991 when hikers found the mummified body of a man who died there 5,000 years ago. Although not a true fossil, the "Iceman," as he is called, was so perfectly preserved in the ice that scientists can tell much about him. The Iceman was in his late twenties or thirties. He wore animal skins, a grass cape, and leather shoes. In his hand, this mysterious stranger from the past still clutched an ax.

New fossils are being found all the time. They continue to tell us many things about the earth. But there is still so much to learn.

Hadrosaurs
(duckbills)

Did other giant creatures roam the earth? What really happened to the dinosaurs and other prehistoric animals? What were early people like?

Someday we hope to learn the answers to these questions. Fossils will give us the clues and help show the way. What treasures will we find on the path to discovery?

Only time will tell! Meanwhile the search for answers—and fossils—continues.

Protoceratops